WE'RE ALL LIARS

101 Ways to Live the Truth

By Robert Biehn

ISBN: 978-0-578-60864-8

First Edition

Printed in the United States of America

Robert Biehn
Murfreesboro, TN, 37130
info@robertbiehn.com

Dedicated to my wife, Stephanie Biehn, who helps me to be a more honest man each and every day. I love you. Thank you.

CONTENTS

PREFACE
ADMITTING THE TRUTH: WE ARE ALL LIARS

Hello! Thank you for picking up this book. I'm sure that if you're reading this one of two things triggered your interest:

1. You saw this book and its design or title caught your attention. If so, that's great! Because if you think the look or title is unique, then I think you'll find that the *feel* and contents of this book are quite unique as well.
2. You picked up this book because you hate being lied to. I suspect that you, like me, and millions of others (perhaps everyone in this world) hate being lied to. However, everyone is a liar, but no one has the courage to admit it. Being lied to often seems like an impossible obstacle to overcome in our interactions with others, and so frequently leads to the deterioration of our relationships, even ones we couldn't stand to lose.

We all lie. We all know we all lie. And yet, we still spend so much time pretending we don't lie as much as we do. Why is that? Because our innate fears and society have both convinced us of a fatal ideology: **that lying protects and the truth destroys**. Do you know what's ironic? The only thing that the truth destroys is lies. For everything else, the truth sets us free.

This book is separated into three parts:

1. The first part is to get us to admit that we're all liars. We lie every day and more often than we realize.
2. The second part is a breakdown of the truths behind some of the most common white lies we hear and say every day, and the true statements we could say instead.
3. The third part is a challenge aimed at helping us discover that being honest with ourselves and others is essential to living a happy, fulfilling life.

Why are these important? Because lies, whether they are from a loved one, a co-worker, a boss, an officer, a politician, or a post on social media, are destructive in their very nature. Yet, what if we could completely get rid of lies in our lives? What would that feel like to you? I bet it'd be a relief. You'd no longer have to play guessing games with people or wonder what someone's intentions really are. You'd know right away. Granted, it'd be painful at times, but, in the long run, don't you think knowing the truth is better than being lied to? Now, we all know there's no possible way to completely eliminate lies. However, I will say this: **you can compel honesty *without* even asking for it**. How do you do that? Simple: **stop lying to yourself**. In other words, tell yourself the truth even when you don't want to hear it. When you start to do that, then you'll start to see a shift within your relationships. Honesty becomes a currency you offer to others, and in return, you'll receive honesty (or in the least, greater clarity).

I bet you're wondering the big question "Is being honest, even about the little things, really that important?" The short answer is a resounding "Yes!" Let me put it another way, though.

When we are born we are given a glass tray. Smooth, clear, and without flaws. As we grow, our relationships with others are stacked on that glass tray. From underneath we look up through the glass to see those relationships, as well as the reflection of ourselves. Every lie, even "small" or "white" lies we deem harmless, put a chip into that glass. Of course, the first chip won't cause the glass to shatter, but it will slightly hinder our ability to see our relationships clearly, including the one with ourselves that we see in the glass' reflection. As we continue to lie, oftentimes without even realizing it, those harmless "chips" from the white lies and the massive cracks from intentional lies start to add up. Now, not only can we not see our relationships clearly because of the damage we have done to the glass, but our own perception of ourselves is lost in all the chips and cracks. At any point, one tiny, minuscule lie can cause everything to come crashing down. **Don't lose hope**. The truth is a powerful force, and while the truth can't turn back time or undo lies, it can fill in the cracks and chips and strengthen your tray that could be one chip away from shattering. But, the truth requires steady, daily execution, and must always be handled with care. If you stick with it, though, you will gain clarity to see yourself and those around you in a way you had forgotten was possible. False perceptions will crumble around you. Your words will exemplify both love and respect. Ultimately, you will become absolute, even in times of uncertainty, and you will breathe easy knowing that you are guided by the pursuit and application of truth.

This book is focused on helping us to be honest with ourselves, and in turn, honest with others. It's not easy, I know, especially since society typically encourages us to be polite liars and make excuses. Yet, is that what you want? Be *honest*, do you really want a life built on polite lies and misleading intentions? If you honestly do, then this book might not be for you (but I still encourage you to read it or give it to someone else.) However, if you want a life centered on honesty, where the truth is prevalent and becomes your fuel, rather than your burden, a powerful force that moves people and refines yourself and your relationships, then this is the book for you.

Still need another reason to keep reading? Do you like winning? Because the truth wins 100% of the time, **in love, in business, in everything.**

We're All Liars is filled with bite-sized suggestions that have a deep meaning packed into them. Some are easy to digest, while others might require a little extra chewing. Some may be reminders, while others may be revelations. All of them are applicable and relevant to everyone.

A couple of important notes about this book:

1. When gender is specified from a male's perspective (my own) please note that it is applicable to everyone.
2. When the lines have "you" in them, please understand that it is because these are meant to encourage us to first look at ourselves and how these might apply to our own lives, and then others. It is not the assumptive judgment of you as the person you are. Only you can judge that (if you are honest with yourself).
3. They are in no particular order, and are meant to be read every day, or pulled out when you run into complex situations, or to be used as helpful suggestions to give to others.
4. Each line, even if it does not seem to be directly linked to you, is for your benefit.
5. Toward the end of the book we will have an interactive part, an "Opportunity" section which addresses some of the most common "white lies" we tell ourselves. First, it will break down the truths that are behind those lies, and then it will give some suggestions on how to express those truths as opposed to lying. There will be blank spaces throughout to give you a chance to write down your own truths if it is not listed. I strongly encourage you to do each one of them. This will help you to be able to catch the lies you may not even be aware of in yourself and others.

If this book moves you, then I encourage you to get one for someone you know. I'd also love to see you post some of your favorite lines on social media so we can share it with others. After all, who couldn't use a little more honest encouragement in their lives? I happen to love letters as well, so I'd be so glad to hear from you! And of course, if you have questions, send them my way too! To the best of my abilities, I am here for you.

Thank you for this opportunity to share my honesty with you. I hope that it blesses your life in some way.

Sincerely,
Robert Biehn
info@robertbiehn.com

P.S: I am sure that there are several of these you may disagree with, and I completely respect that and hope that these will inspire you to seek the truth of your own life. This book is not an end-all solution, nor do I regard it as a complete guide. Instead, I hope it is a stepping stone, a point of inspiration that sparks or fuels your internal growth towards becoming more honest with yourself and others.

Now then, let's **be** ***honest...***

...we're all liars.

PART 1: THINGS TO CONSIDER

1. Don't let your politeness come out in the form of a lie.

In others words: Do you think "white lies" are okay? They are not. A lie is a lie, no matter the intention behind it.

It's better to temporarily hurt someone with the truth than lose them forever when your lies are exposed.

Don't let your politeness come out in the form of a lie.

2. You'll never learn to be honest and fair if your process for handling difficult or serious matters is simply to avoid those necessary interactions.

◆ ◆ ◆

3. Don't do something for someone because they are attractive, rich, or hold a position of power. Do it to be of service to them.

After all, wealth, titles, and other material items come and go, as will your relationship with those people; but, if you do something to help someone else, then that will be a timeless reward for you and them, no matter the circumstances of life.

◆ ◆ ◆

4. Don't let the potential of being rejected keep you away from pursuing something or someone. However, if rejection does occur, have respect for that rejection and don't try to force something that the other person doesn't want.

For example: If you love a woman and you tell her "I love you", as long as it's respectful, there's nothing wrong with that. You're just being honest and sincere. However, if she was to ask you to stop expressing such things, then if you truly love her you will stop. Why? Because love is selfless, not selfish. So, if you were honest in saying you "love" her, show it by respecting her rejection.

◆ ◆ ◆

5. Questions don't hurt, but miscommunications do.

If someone implies something, clarify. Your understanding may be entirely different than their intention.

6. Rejection is not a negative thing; it is the end of a distraction and the beginning of a new opportunity.

◆ ◆ ◆

7. Be honest with yourself about your intentions, but do not let your intentions become obsessions.

Why does this matter? It matters because honest intentions behind our motives are great, but often we let our honest intentions become obsessions. This creates dishonest circumstances that could lead to very harmful consequences.

◆ ◆ ◆

8. Bragging is a sign that your character is lacking. Be honest, but humble.

For example: which do you think commands the awe and inspiration from others? The man who walks into the room and has to convince everyone that he is someone important? Or the man who walks into a room and everyone knows there is merit and worth to his name by the reputation he holds and the way he carries himself?

◆ ◆ ◆

9. Learn to appreciate who is directly in front of you.

It is impossible to accurately compare one person to another; our circumstances are individually unique.

◆ ◆ ◆

10. If you do something nice for someone, do it without the expectation of a thank you or another form of gratitude.

Be honest with yourself and remember they didn't ask you to do anything, to begin with, you chose to do it.

◆ ◆ ◆

11. Think before you speak, shallow words make relationships weak.

In other words: Don't make promises or say things that you are not able to or don't intend to fulfill. Your relationship will be nothing more than a balloon of air, and while it will seems to be soaring high, all it will take is one little prick of a needle to cause it to pop.

◆ ◆ ◆

12. How you treat those who offend you will prove how easily your love will break or bend.

◆◆◆

13. A relationship is not a win, like receiving a trophy to put on a shelf. It is a title of trust that you wear each and every day.

◆◆◆

14. If you talk a lot, learn to listen. The more you talk, the less you know.

How can you possibly be a good partner, co-worker, spouse, or friend if you know nothing about the other person?

◆ ◆ ◆

15. Holding hands is fine, as long as both people know what it really means. One may think a relationship is building, while the other may consider it a casual expression of affection.

◆ ◆ ◆

16. Kisses are promises of the lips. Only give them if you can faithfully, fully, commit.

◆◆◆

17. If you've newly met, don't read into their texts.

Be honest with your assumptions because written messages lack tone and intention and are often full of misunderstandings.

◆ ◆ ◆

18. Only ask her on a date when you're at peace with any fate.

If you want your relationship to be honest, it needs to have honest and clear intentions from the very beginning.

◆◆◆

19. If you buy someone a present, make sure it fits your current level of relationship with them.

For example: if you're just friends with a girl, then buying her roses, heart-shaped boxes of chocolate, and giving romantic cards doesn't fit your relationship of being friends. Don't mislead yourself or them, because that will lead to severe disappointment.

◆ ◆ ◆

20. If they're an ex, don't treat them any less. Not worst, not best, just like the rest.

In other words: just because you have a painful past with someone doesn't mean you should treat them poorly in the present. Now, that's not saying you have to go out of your way to be kind to them either. Simply treat them as you would any other person that you meet.

◆ ◆ ◆

21. Harm befalls both sides when we make old enemies into future foes.

In other words: let's say your co-worker and you have had a rocky altercation. The next time you see them, don't immediately begin from that negative place you left off at. All you'd be doing is guaranteeing yourself another enemy.

For example: let's say you had an ex who you felt treated you poorly. You broke up, haven't seen them in years, and then run into them. Instead of immediately looking at them as an enemy, which creates stress and hostility in both your lives, try to look at them as a stranger you are meeting again.

◆ ◆ ◆

22. Compliments are like salt: a little bit adds to the moment, but too much ruins the dish.

Only give compliments out if they are completely honest and your intentions for them are honest as well.

◆ ◆ ◆

23. If you want your love to have depth and meaning, then make sure your "I love you" holds the weight of true love, not just situational affection.

For example: in the Latin language there are 7 different types of love, they are...

i. Eros – sexual or passionate love.
ii. Philia – friendship or shared goodwill.
iii. Storge – familial love (family).
iv. Agape – universal love, love for all things.
v. Ludus – playful or uncommitted love.
vi. Pragma – practical, reasonable love.
vii. Philautia – self-love.

The point of all that is to make it abundantly clear that even thousands of years ago there was a deep understanding that "love" is often backed by temperamental, situational, dutiful, or otherwise biased reasons. Be aware and honest about the reason you "love" someone.

◆ ◆ ◆

24. Don’t let yourself be fooled by occasional kindness. Honest emotions tell a steady truth.

◆ ◆ ◆

25. Money is not the de-termination of wealth.

In other words: we have to drive ourselves into the core of what truly makes us feel satisfied and successful. If you are poor, but you still find reasons to be thankful, then you are abundantly wealthy, because even the richest among us typically find themselves penniless when it comes to happiness.

◆ ◆ ◆

26. Always try to be considerate because forgetting consideration will become a habit that will only worsen over time.

For example: When you forget to thank someone, to ask someone how they are, it becomes commonplace to be negligent of your thoughtfulness. People will start to feel you don't care about them, that you take things for granted, and you might find yourself forgetting that other people exist (their lives, emotions, feelings). Soon after, you may find that people don't want to be around you because you seem to have no appreciation for them.

27. Whatever your faith, just remember there is a time, a way, and a place to express its truths in good taste.

◆◆◆

28. A true friend doesn't lie.

In other words: if you had to pick between saying an important truth to your friend or risking your friendship, tell them the truth. A true friend values the well-being of their friends more than their friendships.

◆ ◆ ◆

29. Be patient.

In other words: be patient.

For example: be patient.

Seriously though...this is probably one of the hardest realities for us to face in life. Everything about our world tells us to be impatient, but if we are to be honest with history, patience has always prevailed. In business, we admire those who built empires, not those who rose and fell in a day. In relationships, we speak highly of marriages and friendships that last ages. So, remember the 3 P's: proactive, productive, patient.

◆ ◆ ◆

30. Don't be subtle or back-handed, be open and understanding.

In other words: you're not going to get anywhere by making sly comments or backhanded insults. Either choose to speak your truths in a respectful manner so you can find a resolution, or keep your discontentment to yourself and come to peace with the present circumstances.

◆ ◆ ◆

31. Be wary of saying "yes" because you're impressed.

In other words: when we are impressed by someone, whether it is their knowledge, looks, wealth, whatever, we tend to let our guard down and quickly agree or make decisions because we are impressed, not because we logically reasoned out our choices.

◆ ◆ ◆

32. Be wary of saying "no" before you "know".

In other words: we all judge. It's a factual and unavoidable truth. What is important is what we do with our judgments. It's okay to see someone who looks sketchy and say "that person looks sketchy" and do some minor, practical things to respond to our reason. What isn't okay is to deem someone who looks "sketchy" as less of a human. Just because someone isn't wearing a suit, doesn't mean they are unsuccessful. Just because someone is overweight, doesn't mean that they are irresponsible. ONE surface judgment should not dictate your total view of who a person is.

◆ ◆ ◆

33. If you are obsessed with finding something better, you will never find something that is enough.

◆ ◆ ◆

34. Purpose is not casual.

For example: if you say you feel your purpose in life is to do music for a living or become a teacher, but you don't do anything to pursue those on a CONSISTENT basis, then do not let yourself be surprised when you feel you don't have any "purpose". Purpose is not casual.

◆ ◆ ◆

35. To know one, you must not be distracted by many.

In other words: though this contradicts popular belief in dating apps, if you want to find someone that you deeply connect with, then spending hours texting/messaging multiple people splits your ability to focus, which splits your ability to LEARN and actually get to know someone. Now, does that mean you can't talk to multiple people? Of course not. But if your honest goal is to find that "special" someone, then don't you think that will require special attention? If you're honest with yourself and others, then knowing who to give special attention to will become increasingly clear. If you start to invest attention into them and they turn out not to be who you thought, then be honest with yourself and adjust your attention and focus appropriately. The truth is, we only have a small amount of focus that we can give to relationships.

◆ ◆ ◆

36. Devotion does not mean isolation, but rather, selective dedication. The difference is worth its weight in gold.

◆◆◆

37. When first meeting: though her eyes may captivate, save your gaze for a later date.

In other words: even if you feel truly connected to someone when you first meet them, be wise and patient. Don't spend your early interactions romanticizing them because it will cloud your judgment and ability to learn who they are.

◆ ◆ ◆

38. It is better to be overwhelmed by the truth than to be comfortable in a lie.

◆ ◆ ◆

39. Admiration and infatuation are often difficult to tell apart.

◆ ◆ ◆

40. Perhaps someone's or something's rejection is God's protection.

◆◆◆

41. A man that boasts of human credentials and awards as the basis of his spiritual worth, is a man who knows not the currency of the soul. He has been bought by, and consequently owned by, the circumstances of his material situations.

◆ ◆ ◆

42. Always seek to find the root, don't be tantalized by the fruit.

In other words: just because an opportunity looks sweet, delicious, or promising, doesn't mean it actually is. The next time you see an opportunity, challenge yourself to figure out why that opportunity is there, and why that opportunity exists for you.

For example: and this is a lighthearted example...but often times you'll see job ads claiming "earn 6 figures" and "work for a Fortune 500 Company" and "entry-level". You get excited about this opportunity, go in for an interview, and you learn that the job is selling cell phone plans outside of a 99-cent store. Now, technically they didn't lie, as the big cell phone companies are Fortune 500 companies, and if you sell enough phones/plans you could, in fact, acquire a six-figure income. This isn't to say you shouldn't do those jobs or take opportunities. Instead, be honest with yourself and make sure to not be distracted by the appearance and promise of something.

◆ ◆ ◆

43. "Good" is not confined to the limits of our minds.

In other words: it's so easy for us to make excuses or find reasons to be miserable. It's human nature. We place so much trust in material things and situations that when something or a series of events don't go the way we plan that it's just "bad luck" or "it's just not my day". Yet, the mind-frame of viewing anything that doesn't go our way as "bad" will keep us in a never-ending cycle of misery. I'll say it again: "Good" is not confined to the limits of our minds.

◆ ◆ ◆

44. Do not allow the priceless gift of love to be bought with the inflated currency of words.

◆ ◆ ◆

45. It is impossible to pour from an empty cup.

In other words: Only a heart that is fulfilled can help to fill another heart.

◆ ◆ ◆

46. Just because you "win" someone over doesn't mean that they are "the one".

◆◆◆

47. Concerns should be addressed before saying "yes".

For example: Two people want to get married, but know they have opposite beliefs. Instead of saying "love will triumph", which many divorced marriages have said, address the serious and potential marriage-ending issues **before** you get married.

◆ ◆ ◆

48. If you're not married to them, don't act as if you are.

In other words: Marriage isn't a play. It's not acting. It's real and genuine. Which means that if you're not married to them, don't pretend to be.

◆ ◆ ◆

49. Deceit is easily conceived when we are desperate to receive.

In other words: If you are desperate for love, you may find yourself with someone who does not love you.

For example: I'm sure you've heard people say "We just fell out of love" or "One day I realized I didn't love them anymore." Here's the thing, that cannot be true. What would be better translated would be one of two things:

1. They never loved them to begin with and were instead desperate for something other than love, and finally realized that.

2. They loved things about them (sex, company, laughing, etc.) but did not love them as a whole.

This is so because love also means "truth" and it is boundless. Don't let that confuse you though, as you can love someone but very much dislike them.

Challenge: Next time you think of saying "I love you" to them, think of whether your words and actions reflect the truth of what it really means to say "I love you". For a good definition, I recommend 1 Corinthians 13: 4-8.

◆ ◆ ◆

50. Honest and sincere appreciation will beget results that criticism and ridicule cannot.

◆ ◆ ◆

*51. When you want something from someone, engage them with **their** interests, not your own.*

52. Any man can be a millionaire, for the value of money is an imaginary currency that is printed, regulated and managed by other men.

◆◆◆

53. Learn to love, respect, and appreciate someone without the expectations of material return.

◆ ◆ ◆

54. When you've been broken down enough, you become skilled at building back up.

55. A man must focus first on his character, then his conduct will surely follow.

◆ ◆ ◆

56. We should not look for someone else if we have not first come to terms with who we were, who we honestly are, and who we want to be.

In other words: Don’t go looking for someone else if you haven't found yourself.

◆ ◆ ◆

57. Don't want an answer so badly that you're willing to accept a lie.

◆ ◆ ◆

58. You will not see a meaningful transformation in your life unless you are entirely committed to making it happen. You will not have the necessary commitment until you realize the need for change.

◆◆◆

59. Happiness is the residual reward of responsibility.

Happiness is not bought, it is not gifted, it is not contingent upon the world or people satisfying desires. Happiness is found in the individual pursuit of the truth.

◆ ◆ ◆

60. Heroes are just people who decided to save someone who couldn't save themselves. You can be a hero.

For example: Have you ever heard the phrase "the truth sets you free"? Well, when we think of victims, we think of people who are powerless, oppressed, enslaved, and so on. When interacting with others, giving respectful honesty is a way to help set them free from your own lack of truthfulness.

In other words: every single time you lie to someone, you are the villain, not the hero.

◆ ◆ ◆

61. True love isn't contingent upon your belief in it. It is an absolute universal truth.

◆ ◆ ◆

62. One of the quickest ways to express your love for another is to express love for whatever is closest to their heart.

◆ ◆ ◆

63. It is much better to own a few things than to owe on many things. One is an owner, the other a slave.

In other words: We have been terribly lied to on this subject. We're encouraged to get ourselves into staggering amounts of student debt, being told that it is a necessary debt for a better life. We have been taught that buying the most expensive phone, constantly going to see the newest movie, playing the newest game, and having the newest clothes, makeup, and so on are all essential parts of living and that we cannot be happy without them. Let me ask you this, and be honest: if you had an extra $10,000 right now, how would that make you feel? If you could use that $10,000 to pay off credit card or other debt, would that bring you relief and even pride? Would it bring you **more** relief than a cup of coffee? Would it bring you **more** pride than the last movie you saw? Please don't think I am saying that you cannot have recreation and do "fun" things. That's not the case at all. I am merely stating that debt crushes our spirits, blocks our abilities to live freely, and ultimately keeps us from our dreams. Debt will occur, for most all of us, but we can take charge and limit how much debt. Less debt = more financial **AND** emotional freedom.

◆ ◆ ◆

64. Prepare for the future, sustain the present, appreciate the past.

65. Pain can often be a protective measure.

If you so choose it, you could become an individual that even when the thorns of mortality prick your finger, you do not dread the bite nor dwell on the pain, but rather keep your attention focused on the rose..

For example: Let's say you were with someone that you dearly cared about and then for whatever reason that relationship ended and you never fulfilled those dreams of marrying them and living your life with them. In the moment that will feel like a crushing blow, which it is. It's awful, painful, and so much more. Yet, that pain is more than likely protecting us from a lifetime of misery.

◆ ◆ ◆

66. Consequences are opportunities for us to grow and refocus on what matters most.

◆◆◆

67. Failure only lingers in a lazy mind.

◆◆◆

68. Being honest should not lead you into compromising situations, it should lead you out of them.

◆◆◆

69. Our advice to others should be based on questions that lead them to reason out truthful answers of their own.

In other words: there is no possible way for you to know what is best for someone else. All you can do is support them and help them to discover their own truths.

◆ ◆ ◆

70. "Yes" and "no" should not be based on impulsive feelings, but rather practiced reasoning and experiences.

◆◆◆

71. If you want to make an impression, listen.

In other words: Polite words are an invitation for a brief interaction. Generally, people don't want to hear our story, they want to tell theirs.

◆ ◆ ◆

72. No matter your relationship to someone, if they have no interest in listening, then do not talk.

◆ ◆ ◆

73. A messenger brings the message exactly as it is written, while a gossiper brings the message written in the ink of personal opinion.

◆ ◆ ◆

74. True equality is not about equal outcome, but equal opportunity.

◆ ◆ ◆

75. Equal opportunity often looks unequal because individual capabilities and choices beget different results.

◆ ◆ ◆

76. Freedom from responsibility is imagination, while the liberty to manage responsibility is a fact.

◆ ◆ ◆

77. Love isn't contingent upon the person in front of you, but rather, the person within you.

◆ ◆ ◆

78. Your individual worth and value are not based on your opinions or the opinions of others. It is an intangible quality.

79. The moment we give our past to God is the moment it becomes positively relevant to our future.

◆◆◆

80. Every need we have can be met while still helping others to acquire their needs.

◆ ◆ ◆

81. Money is a servant to us in our service to God. Not the other way around.

◆ ◆ ◆

82. Actions are a reflection of faith, but not the definition of it.

◆ ◆ ◆

83. We are unaware of the outcome of any decision we don't make.

◆ ◆ ◆

84. A cage made of lies is not how you keep others close.

◆◆◆

85. Peace is not something we find, but rather, something we allow.

◆ ◆ ◆

86. Just because you are together, doesn't mean you should be.

◆ ◆ ◆

87. Wisdom is knowing that despite everything you know, you still have so much to learn.

In other words: If you're the smartest person in the room, you're not.

◆ ◆ ◆

88. Being factually correct does not mean you are morally right. Being morally right is not a supplement for facts.

◆◆◆

89. If you truly need particular questions answered, then ask them in a way that encourages them to be answered.

For example: If you want to know why someone lied to you, instead of saying "Why did you lie to me?" perhaps say something like "It seems like you're holding back something, what can I do to help you feel more comfortable in sharing more?"

The point is to encourage them, inspire them, and comfort them into sharing the truth. If you try to force them to say the truth, more than likely you'll get another series of lies.

◆ ◆ ◆

90. Solemnity is the foundation from which happiness builds its nest.

In other words: happiness isn't being carefree, fake smiling, saying "everything's okay" or "I'm fine" when you're not. Happiness isn't a façade or a mask that we wear. Happiness is when you can face the truths of life and see how even the things that seem "bad" provide you an opportunity for good that wasn't there before.

For example: getting laid off or fired from a job doesn't equal "bad". It will feel like it, of course, and it will be scary and tough. However, it is an opportunity to refocus on what matters most in your life. Maybe your current job didn't allow you to spend time with your family, maybe you were looking to move, maybe the job encouraged bad habits, maybe you always wanted to pursue a different career, the list goes on. Do you see how one "bad" thing, getting fired, opened up so many opportunities for good that weren't directly available?

To recap: getting hurt, getting fired, getting sick, and so on are all crummy things to go through. You don't need to fake a smile and say "I'm fine". Face them for what they are: painful, but new opportunities to focus on what really matters.

◆ ◆ ◆

91. Happiness is born from the pursuit of truth, while joy thrives on the application of truth.

◆◆◆

92. Only a foolish man wastes his time gazing upon the things he wishes to buy but cannot presently afford.

In other words: window shopping, daydreaming about riches, etc. are the very things that will distract you from obtaining what you want.

◆ ◆ ◆

93. A foolish man is persistent without reason, while a wise man is persistent to gain reason.

For example: I'm sure you've heard someone say "On that grind" or "gotta hustle". Yet, if you ask them why, their response tends to be something shallow, like money, sex, a title, or some other endless chase that has nothing to do with being happier, kinder, or otherwise improving THEMSELVES, not just their material lives.

◆ ◆ ◆

94. Your conviction is only as strong as your reason.

In other words: if your goal is to buy a watch, then your conviction is only as big as that watch. However, if your goal is to have the financial freedom to support yourself, your family, and help others, then your commitment becomes as strong as your love for them.

95. Wishing for our past to change denies our growth in the present and future.

◆ ◆ ◆

96. Heartbreak is not defeat, but rather an opportunity to understand the definition of true love.

◆ ◆ ◆

97. Butterflies in our stomach have nothing to do with the love in our heart.

◆◆◆

98. In silence we learn to hear that which is unspoken.

◆ ◆ ◆

99. Laziness is a deceitful friend, while preparedness is a constant ally.

◆◆◆

100. There is never such a thing as bad in life, but only the good we have yet to understand.

◆ ◆ ◆

101. Above all else the integrity of the truth must be preserved.

◆◆◆

PART 2: SOCIETY IS A LIAR

Let's Work it Out

The truths behind white lies are opportunities to become more honest.

Below are white lies that we commonly use. Some of them may be true, but I'm sure as you read them you will discover how frequently they have been used as lies, both intentionally and unintentionally. I am going to address some of these and then offer 'Opportunity Phases' at the end of each one for you to use next time you find yourself wanting to say them. You can also fill in the blanks with your own truths and opportunity phrases. Remember, these are not just for your interactions with others, but also for how you speak and talk about yourself and life.

I love ~~you~~.

Truth: *I love…*

... not being alone.

...feeling secure.

...attention.

____

Opportunity:

- "Thank you for being here for me."
- "I am grateful for your comfort."
- "I appreciate the affection you show me."

____

Do you *actually* love them? **Be honest**: ______________

I hate ~~you~~.

Truth: *I hate...*

... when you say that.

... when you do that.

...the choices you make.

...that you have something I don't.

____

Opportunity:

- "I do not appreciate it when you say [insert hurtful words]."

- "I am hurt when you do/say those things."

- "I dislike the way you choose to live your life."

- "One day I'd like to have [insert jealousy reason]."

____

Do you *actually* hate them? **Be honest**: ________________

I hate ~~myself~~.

Truth: *I hate my...*

... choices.

... attitude.

... situation.

____

Opportunity:

- "I am not proud of the decisions I have made."
- "I do not like my outlook on life."
- "I am unhappy with my current circumstances."

____

Do you *actually* hate yourself? **Be honest**: ____________

I'm short on cash.

I've got nothing on me.

-When the homeless ask you for money, are you actually short on cash? Or do you just not trust them with the money?

- If you give to someone, whether they are homeless, a friend, church, charity, anyone, do so with the understanding that you are doing this to give. It's not about money, it's about giving first.

- If you tell people you are short on cash, make sure that it is honest. Don't say you're short on cash because you don't want to pay. If someone invites you out and you're actually short on cash, then be honest while still expressing your care for them. If you tell people you are short on cash to get them to pay things for you, know that it will **ALWAYS** cost you more in the end. A lifetime of relationships is not worth a couple of movie tickets, sandwiches, coffees, whatever.

Truth:

-I don't trust you to use this money wisely.

-I don't want to spend money on that [thing they want to do].

-I don't want to pay.

____

Opportunity:

- "I would love to spend time with you, but right now I'm short on cash."

- "Thanks for inviting me, but right now I need to be saving, so maybe you'd like to [insert alternative, affordable idea]."

- "To be honest, I'm just not in a place to spend [or give] financially. Is there some other way I can bless you today?"

____

Are you *actually* short on cash? **Be honest**: ___________

I'm here for you.

-This one is difficult because we often use it to comfort people. It is one I've struggled with plenty. I think prefacing what you mean, what you are offering, is best. Help set the expectations of what you can realistically give because the last thing someone in distress needs is overpromising and under-delivering.

Truth:

- I want to help you, but I'm caught up in my own situations.

- I have empathy for your circumstances.

- I don't know what to say, but I care.

____

Opportunity:

- "I am here for you. Text me anytime."

- "I work a lot, but I am here for you whenever I can be."

- "I know we're far apart, but you can reach out when you need me and I'll respond as soon as I can."

- "I don't know how I can help you, but I care and hope everything is resolved."

____

Are you *actually* there for them? **Be honest**: ___________

No ~~offense~~...

Truth: *No...*

...respect or regard for how your opinion may affect someone else.

...humility for the fact you might not be right or it isn't your place to tell/speak.

...desire to be helpful, only to have control, the last word.

____

Opportunity:

- "I don't think this is a subject I should be commenting on. It's not really my place."

- "I would be glad to tell you my honest opinion, but understand it's just an opinion."

- "I'd like to give you an appropriate response, so I'm going to take a little time to think about it and then I will get back to you."

____

Do you *actually* mean no offense? **Be honest**: __________

Let's keep in touch.

- People often want to feel connected to others, but so often we also say "let's keep in touch" when we don't mean it. Generally, we do this to avoid hurting someone's feelings for a multitude of reasons.

Truth:

- I did not enjoy our time, but I don't want to hurt your feelings.

- I enjoyed our time together, but I don't want to commit to something I can't fulfill.

- You seem like a nice person, but I realized that I just don't want to invest more time.

____

Opportunity:

Business:

- "I appreciate what you shared with me today, but I'm not in a place for utilizing what you are offering. If that changes, I will be sure to reach out."

____

Friends/Strangers:

- "I enjoyed connecting with you today."
- "It was a pleasure meeting you, I'll see you around!"
- "Thanks for hanging out with me today."

____

Do you *actually* want to keep in touch? **Be honest**: _____

I ~~forgot.~~

I got stuck in traffic, my alarm didn't go off, I didn't see your message, etc.

Truth: *I...*

...don't care.

...had more important things on my mind.

...did not set reminders.

... was distracted.

____

Opportunity:

- "I didn't set reminders, and I'm sorry. I'll be more prepared next time."

- "I committed to this but had something that needed my immediate attention. I'm sorry for any inconvenience this caused you."

- "I honestly forgot, and that's not a reflection of my care for you, it's just something I am working on getting better at. I am sorry."

- "Thank you for your patience."

____

Did you *actually* forget? **Be honest:** _____________________

I already have plans.

Im busy, I'm booked up.

Truth:

- You are not a priority to me.
- I don't want to do the things you want to do.
- I'm tired, but I don't want to hurt your feelings.

____

Opportunity:

- "I have things I need to focus my attention on right now."
- "I'd like to spend time with you, but I honestly just don't want to do [insert their idea]. Would you be willing to do something else with me?"
- "I'm tired and I just really want to rest."
- "Would you be willing to reschedule for another time? I just have more going on than I realized."

____

Do you *actually* have plans? **Be honest**: _______________

Looks ~~don't~~ matter.

Truth: *Looks [don't] matter.*

- Looks **DO** matter.

- Looks aren't the most important part, but they are important.

- I do care about what you look like, but I care **more** about who you are as a person.

- Looks are all I care about.

____

Opportunity:

- "I'm attracted to you, but I'm also attracted to who you are as a person."

- "You are so beautiful (handsome), and I also really appreciate how you treat me too."

- "Looks are a bonus, but the prize is our relationship."

____

Do looks *actually* not matter? **Be honest**: ______________

I'd be happy to.

Truth:

- I *am* obligated to help.

- I *feel* obligated to help.

- I don't want to do this, but I will because I don't want you to think I'm a selfish person if I don't.

- I want something in return for helping.

____

Opportunity:

- "No problem, I'd be glad if someone helped me."

- "I've only got [insert time-frame] but I'll do what I can."

- "I can do [insert request] but then I have to get going."

- "I'm not in a position to take this on myself, but I can help you find someone who can."

- "I have immediate matters I have to take care of first, but I can help you once they are finished."

- "I can't do that."

____

Are you *actually* happy to help? **Be honest**: __________

I'll See.
Maybe, I'll Check.

Truth: *I'll...*

...avoid this topic from this point on because I don't want to deal with it but I can't bring myself to say no.

...keep putting it off because I don't want to let you down, but I can't or won't do this.

- I have no confidence at all that this will work out, but I'll put the minimal amount of effort into trying.

- I'm only doing this because I don't want you to get upset at me.

____

Opportunity:

- "I'm really not sure right now, and I don't want to commit to something."

- "I appreciate the offer, but I'm not really in a position to commit to anything. If that changes, I'll be sure to reach out."

- "I'm not sure this is going to work with what I have going on, but I'll check and give you an honest answer."

____

Will you *actually* see? **Be honest**: ______________________

It wasn't my fault.

Truth:

- I don't want to accept responsibility for my actions.
- I was involved, but I feel my actions were justified.
- I think someone else is more responsible than I am in this situation.
- I don't want to help you because this has nothing to do with me.

____

Opportunity:

- "I am sorry. This was my fault."
- "This was an unintentional mistake. I'll work to not let it happen again."
- "I wasn't involved in this, but I'll help as best as I can."

____

Was it *actually* not your fault? **Be honest**: _____________

I ~~love~~ it!

Truth: *I [love] it!*

- I like it, not love it.
- I don't think it's a great idea, but I don't want to hurt your feelings since you seem excited about it.
- I'm not confident in this idea, but I don't have a better one, so I'll go with yours.

____

Opportunity:

- "I think it's worth looking into."
- "In my opinion, it's pretty good, but I think we could come up with some other options too."
- "I think this is the best idea we've had so far!"

____

Do you *actually* love it? **Be honest**: ____________________

I miss ~~you~~.
We should hangout.

Truth: *I miss...*

...having company.

...being comforted.

- I have no one else to spend time with.
- I'm bored.
- I need to ask a favor.
- I want someone listen to me.

____

Opportunity:

- "Would you like to hang out? I enjoy your company."
- "I appreciate when we get to spend time together."
- "I would really appreciate it if I could share [insert topic] with you."
- "I've got a favor to ask, would you be willing to meet up to talk about it?"

____

Do you *actually* miss them? **Be honest**: ______________

I'm over them.

Truth:

- I don't want to admit I'm not over them.
- I'm pretending that I'm not hurting right now.
- I'm angry and my pride is hurt.

____

Opportunity:

- "Right now, I haven't moved on yet."
- "I don't want to be with them anymore, but I'm still really hurting."
- "I'm angry, and my pride is hurt."

____

Are you *actually* over them? **Be honest**: _____________

I want to go to college.

I need a degree.

Truth: *I want...*

...direction.

...to buy time before facing reality.

...to feel secure.

...to please my parents.

- I'm not ready to be on my own.

____

Opportunity:

- "I'm afraid if I don't have a degree I won't succeed in life."

- "I'm hoping college will help me find my career path."

- "I'm afraid of disappointing my parents or being kicked out or cut off."

- "I can't get my dream job without a degree."

- "I am not confident that my skills and experience alone will be enough."

- "I honestly don't know what else to do."

____

Do you *actually* want to go to college? **Be honest**: ______

I have read the terms and conditions (for jobs, purchases, services, etc.).

Truth:

- Are you kidding me? I'm not going to read all that.

____

Opportunity:

- "I'm going to read all that."
- "I'm not going to read all that and I'm willing to accept the potential consequences of that decision and will not be angry at policies, legal requirements, or other obligations/intrusions that may surprise me but were laid out in the terms and conditions."

____

Did you *actually* read the terms and conditions?
Be honest: ________________________

I don't ~~know~~.

Truth: *I don't...*

...want to tell you the truth.

...want to think about it.

...want to be involved in this.

...care.

____

Opportunity:

- "Great question, I am going to get that answer to you as soon as possible."
- "I am not in a place to answer that question."
- "I'm concerned that answering this will cause more issues rather than give solutions."

____

Do you *actually* not know? **Be honest**: ________________

I don't care.

Truth:

- I do care, I just don't want to admit it.
- I don't know how to express what I'm feeling.
- I feel embarrassed I don't have more to say about this.

____

Opportunity:

- "I need a little more time to give you my opinion."
- "I think that [insert truth]."
- "I don't have a strong enough opinion on this, so I'll leave it up to you."

____

Do you *actually* not care? **Be honest**: _________________

This is the first time this has happened.

Truth:

- I'm ashamed of how many times this has happened.
- I don't want to tell you how many times this has happened because it might keep you from giving me what I want.
- I'm afraid of what you'll think about me if you knew this has happened before.

____

Opportunity:

- "This is private for me."
- "It's happened before, and I am working on making sure it won't happen again."
- "Why is it important for you to know whether this has happened before?"

____

Is this *actually* the first time? **Be honest**: ____________

We're ~~best~~ friends.

Truth:

- We're barely friends.
- We're enemies who pretend to be friends.
- We're not best friends but we say we are because we don't know if we could find another friend.
- We're not best friends, but we are friends.
- Our friendship is convenient.

____

Opportunity:

- "We're friends."
- "I appreciate our friendship so much."
- "I don't think saying a friend is 'best' makes sense."
- "You've put a lot into our friendship, and I appreciate it."
- "We don't get along, but I still want to be respectful toward you."

____

Are you *actually* best friends? **Be honest**: _____________

You look ~~great~~.

Truth: *You look...*

...alright, but not great.

...awful.

...like you could use some help, or sleep, or something.

...great, considering your circumstances.

____

Opportunity:

- "As long as you don't have something professional to do, you look fine."

- "You look like you could use some help, or sleep, or something. How can I help?"

- "Honestly, I think [insert respectful opinion if they asked for it]."

- "I really like [insert aspect of outfit/look/them that you do like]."

____

Do they *actually* look great? **Be honest**: ________________

I'm not attracted to them.

They're not attractive.

Truth:

- They are attractive.
- I think they're more physically attractive than you.
- I don't want to hurt our relationship by saying I'm attracted to them.
- I'm embarrassed that I'm attracted to them.

____

Opportunity:

- "They do have attractive features, but they are not as attractive as you."
- "To be honest, I am a bit jealous of how attractive they are."
- "You are the most attractive person to me."
- "I'm not attracted to their looks, but I can appreciate their personality."

____

Are you *actually* not attracted to them?
Be honest: ____________

It was on sale.

I can afford it, it's just [insert dollar amount].

Truth:

- I really wanted this, but felt I needed an excuse to buy it.
- It wasn't on sale.
- It was on sale, but I knew it was marked up, and I still bought it.
- I can't afford this.
- I'm buying this to bring me temporary satisfaction even though afterward I'll feel guilty.
- I'm in denial of my financial situation.
- I'm unwilling to do what it takes to mend my financial situation.

____

Opportunity (before):

- "I'm going to add this to a list of things I want, but don't need, and won't buy it today."
- "I'm going to wait a few days to see if I still want this."
- "I want this item, but this sale/price is not reasonable, so I'm not going to buy it."
- "I'm going to buy this with the understanding of the effect it will have on my financial situation."

____

Opportunity (after):

- "I'm glad I got this, but since it was more expensive than planned, I'm going to find areas where I can make up for the added cost."

- "This was an emotional purchase. I'm going to return it."

- "It is more expensive than what I was expecting, but I believe it is worth the extra money."

____

Was it *actually* on sale? **Be honest:** ____________________

It's just a white lie.

Trust me, I would never lie to you, I tell the truth, I'm an honest person.

Truth:

- I will lie to you if I feel like it.
- I will lie to you to keep me out of trouble.
- I will lie to avoid hurting you with the truth.
- I will lie to get what I want.
- I will tell you the truth when I can use it to my advantage.
- I will tell you the truth sometimes to make you think I always tell the truth.

____

Opportunity:

- "[insert truth]"
- "I lied, and I'm sorry. The truth is [insert why you lied & tell the truth]"
- "I try to be honest, but sometimes I fall short."

____

Did you lie? **Be honest**: ___________________________

There...you've done it. You've read 101 reminders, ways, revelations, tips on how to live a more honest life. Then, you looked at some of the most common white lies, you broke down their truths, and then you discovered Opportunity Phrases that you can use to become more honest with yourself, with others, and with your life in general. As you learn to address the lies we so often tell ourselves, and others tell us, you will start to find that your life takes a miraculous turn. Suddenly, you'll start to see that you don't hate as many things as you've said do and that when you speak to people, it means something. It's honest, purposeful, and actually puts things in motion, out in the open. Your world will become less dark because your words emit light and invoke truth, rather than masking it and hiding it. You will become incredibly powerful too. It sounds cheesy, but there is absolutely nothing more powerful than the truth. If the truth is the center of your life, if the truth sets us free, then our potential is near limitless.

Thank you for taking the time to read this book. I encourage you to keep it handy with you and read it every day because I think we all know how easy it is to lose sight of the truth. If you felt this benefited you in any capacity, please share it with others. If you had any realizations or your own "Honest Lines", please send them my way! I'd love to feature them and share them with others.

Just know that what you've done here is absolutely incredible. It's miraculous, and also terrifying. You are now not only starting to make yourself a better person, and your life a better life, but you are aiding the world in becoming a better, brighter, more honest place. You are amazing.

Sincerely,
Robert Biehn
info@robertbiehn.com

PART 3: 30 DAYS OF BEING HONEST

Daily Exercise: Uncover the Lies – Recover the Truth

In this next section, we take it a step further. Multiple studies from around the world have concluded that the average person lies quite a lot. But, I bet you didn't need an expansive study to tell you that. You know, just like I know, especially after reading this book, that we all lie, and often more than we realize. Even if they are just "small" lies like saying we "love" someone when we don't, or saying something is "delicious" when it's not, we lie. None of us are perfect. None of us are going to be able to be 100% accurate with our words all the time. That's impossible. Part of becoming more honest in our lives is also becoming more honest about our current abilities. The other part is putting in the effort to become the most honest version of ourselves. Here's where it gets both exciting and brutal at the same time. I encourage you to challenge yourself with "Honest by 30". Each day, for the next 30 days, fill out a page a day about your lies and the truths behind those lies. The goal is to realize how often you lied in a day, why, and what the truth was behind those lies. Here's a real, personal example, to get you started (note: it's a bit vague and names are redacted for privacy. When you fill them in, be detailed, descriptive, and HONEST).

Day 1

Today I Lied _____3_____ times.

My Lies Were:

I lied and said I wanted to catch up with someone when really I just wanted to have an opportunity to mention a project I wanted their help with.

> **Why Did I Lie?** I think I felt guilty that I hadn't reached out to them in a while, and I actually do care about them, but I didn't want them to think I only cared about business.
>
> **What Could I Have Said Instead?** "Hey man, I've got a project going on, and I would really love to share it with you. Is that alright?"

I lied and said I was happy to help someone when I was actually a little annoyed they hadn't taken care of it already.

> **Why Did I Lie?** They had been going through a lot, but also, I knew I was just being selfish. The thing they wanted me to help with took so little effort, and I felt so stupid for acting like it was this big inconvenience.
>
> **What Could I Have Said Instead?** "Sure, I can do that. I know in times like these I always appreciate someone helping me out too."

I lied and said I wasn't frustrated with someone's actions when I brought them a problem to fix and they said there was nothing they could do. I actually was frustrated with their actions and response and just didn't admit it.

> **Why Did I Lie?** I didn't know whether I should be more firm with them or not, and I didn't want to come across as a jerk, just in case I was wrong and there really was nothing they could do about the situation.

What Could I Have Said Instead? "I can see why you would feel that way. I'm frustrated, and I'm not really sure what I should do about it. What do you suggest?"

Day 1

Day 2

Day 3

Day 4

Day 5

Day 6

Day 7

Day 8

Day 9

Day 10

Day 11

Day 12

Day 13

Day 14

Day 15

Day 16

Day 17

Day 18

Day 19

Day 20

Day 21

Day 22

Day 23

Day 24

Day 25

Day 26

Day 27

Day 28

Day 29

Day 30

ABOVE ALL ELSE THE INTEGRITY OF THE TRUTH MUST BE PRESERVED.

Made in the USA
Coppell, TX
09 April 2020

19019331R00098